FAITH LESSONS

IN A

DYNAMITE

GOD

"FOUR DAYS ON THE MOUNTAIN"

By

E. A. JOHNSTON

ISBN: 979-8-9896619-5-4

Printed in the United States of America
January 2024

Formatting and Publishing by
The Old Paths Publications, Inc
4439 Rockrose Green Way
Gainesville, GA 30504
TOP@theoldpathspublications.com
www.theoldpathspublications.com

COVER PHOTO:
"Author atop Pulpit Rock in Ipswich, MA where George Whitefield preached

DEDICATION

The following chapters on the "faith life" are hereby dedicated to:

David Ford, Evangelist

One of the most genuine men of faith I know!

E. A. Johnston
February 2024

PREFACE

Vance Havner once said:

"If we serve such a dynamite God, then how come so many of us are living firecracker lives?"

If that is the case, why aren't we doing greater things for God and making a "bang" in the world for Christ and the Gospel? Is it because we have "firecracker faith"? Or do we have a "big faith" in a big dynamite God? When Jesus was here in His earthly ministry, He asked the searching question: "...*Nevertheless when the Son of man cometh, shall he find faith on the earth?*" (Luke 18:8)?

A book on faith is needed when we need revival; a book on faith is needed when the people of God are discouraged; a book on faith is needed when the Church is weak and powerless. This book is the result of a lifetime of trial and testing, adversity and learning regarding a life of faith. Hopefully, its lessons will strengthen your faith, stretch your faith, and grow your faith. God is looking for faith.

"For the eyes of the LORD run to and fro throughout the whole earth, to shew himself strong in the behalf of them whose heart is perfect toward him" (II Chronicles 16:9).

TABLE OF CONTENTS

DEDICATION 3
PREFACE 5
TABLE OF CONTENTS.......................................7
CHAPTER ONE: HALFHEARTEDNESS 9
CHAPTER TWO: STEPPING OUT ON FAITH 15
CHAPTER THREE: SEEKING FAITH: 21
   FOUR DAYS ON THE MOUNTAIN...................21
      DAY ONE ON THE MOUNTAIN: 23
      DAY TWO ON THE MOUNTAIN:...................24
      DAY THREE ON THE MOUNTAIN: 25
      DAY FOUR ON THE MOUNTAIN: 26
CHAPTER FOUR: ENCOUNTERING GOD 29
    A NEEDED ENCOUNTER........................33
CHAPTER FIVE: FAITH FOR TRAGEDY 37
CHAPTER SIX: THE DAILY QUIET TIME 43
CHAPTER SEVEN: FAITH TESTED 47
CHAPTER EIGHT: MEN OF FAITH............................51
CHAPTER NINE: A SUPER DUPER GOD...................65
CHAPTER TEN: THE PAIN AND GAIN OF FAITH 73
CHAPTER ELEVEN: THE SACRIFICE OF FAITH.......79
CHAPTER TWELVE: FAITH & CROOKED THINGS ...83
CHAPTER THIRTEEN: FAITH TRIED.........................95
CHAPTER FOURTEEN: EMPTY OF SELF................103
CHAPTER FIFTEEN: FAITH AND BROKENNESS....107
CHAPTER SIXTEEN: A DYNAMITE FAITH 113
CHAPTER SEVENTEEN: MAKING OF A MAN OF FAITH
....125
CHAPTER EIGHTEEN: RECOMMENDED READING133
ABOUT THE AUTHOR...135
SOME OF THE BOOKS BY E. A. JOHNSTON..........136

CHAPTER ONE
HALFHEARTEDNESS

"God will not accept a divided heart."

Stephen F. Olford

FAITH LESSON: Halfheartedness to God

BIBLE PASSAGE: II Kings 13:14-19

In II Kings, chapter thirteen, we find the prophet Elisha on his death bed. King Joash, of Israel, comes to pay his last respects. We see this in the following:

> *"Now Elisha was fallen sick of his sickness whereof he died. And Joash the king of Israel came down unto him, and wept over his face, and said, O my father, my father, the chariots of Israel, and the horsemen thereof"* *(verse 14).*

Pictured here is the dying prophet of God and a rotten king, of whom it is said, *"And he did that which was evil in the sight of the LORD"* (II Chronicles 13:11). Yet, the man of God wants to impart a blessing to this king so he can defeat the Syrian army. We take up the striking narrative in the following passage of Scripture:

> *"And Elisha said unto him, Take bow and arrows. And he took unto him bow and arrows. And he said to the king of Israel, Put thine hand upon the bow. And he put his hand upon it: and Elisha put his hands upon the king's hands. And he said, Open the window eastward. And he opened it. Then Elisha said, Shoot. And he shot. And he said, The arrow of the LORD's deliverance, and the arrow of deliverance from Syria: for thou shalt smite the Syrians in Aphek, till thou have consumed them"* (15-17).

What the prophet of God is doing here is illustrating to King Joash that the victory over the Syrian army is symbolized by the arrows of deliverance that he just used as an object lesson. These arrows represent deliverance from the enemies of Israel.

The next two verses are critical to the passage. They represent our Faith Lesson today. Remember the Faith Lesson is Halfheartedness and how we must avoid it at all costs. Pay close attention to the object lesson of faith that Elisha is trying to teach to King Joash:

> *"And he said, Take the arrows. And he took them. And he said unto the king of Israel, Smite upon the ground. And he smote thrice, and stayed. And the man of God was wroth with him, and said, thou shouldest have smitten five or six times; then hadst thou smitten Syria till thou hadst consumed it: whereas now thou shalt smite Syria but thrice"* (18-19).

The great faith lesson here is seen in the number of times that the king of Israel 'should have' struck the ground with the representative handful of arrows. His faith was weak. And because of his weak faith the result ends up as a lost opportunity for God to do more for the people of God in these battles with the Syrian army. We see this truth clearly illustrated in the Gospels about Jesus being hindered by the people's unbelief. *"And he did not many mighty works there because of their unbelief"* (Matthew 13:58).

What our text from II Kings is saying to us is, our faith in a dynamite God is determined by our actions based on that faith! If we step out on faith and believe God and demonstrate that belief by our actions, then God can do big things for us and through us. If we hold back because of unbelief, then God is hindered by that unbelief and lack of faith.

Perhaps some of us are living "firecracker lives" because we would only strike the ground three times, instead of having a bigger faith and striking it six! God wants us to strike it until our arms are worn out! He wants to see our faith in action! Halfheartedness is a result of a lack of faith. And we cannot please God by serving Him with a divided heart! He must have all our whole heart's affections and devotion.

Elisha the man of God was mightily used of God in a dynamite life of faith for God! He did more miracles than his mentor, Elijah! How big is our faith? Given the same circumstances, how many times would we strike the ground with the prophet's arrows? Three? Five? Six?

CHAPTER TWO
STEPPING OUT ON FAITH

"God is looking for the believer who is willing to go out on a limb for Him, to risk everything for Christ and the Gospel."

E. A. Johnston

FAITH LESSON: Stepping out on Faith

BIBLE PASSAGE: Matthew 14:22-31

Our Faith Lesson today is about exercising our faith through the action of stepping out on faith. Whether it is a call to the mission field; a call to full time ministry; a new out of town pastorate; or any challenge that will require you to "step out on faith." My homiletical mentor, Dr. Stephen F. Olford, would always tell me: "What costs counts, and what counts costs!" And that is true whether it is pursuing higher education or learning a new craft or trade. A sacrifice will be involved of time and money and commitment!

Stepping out on faith is a commitment, once made, it must be acted upon and carried out! Our text today is a challenging one, for it demonstrates there is a certain degree of risk involved in stepping out in faith. Here now is our passage of Scripture from Matthew's Gospel in chapter fourteen and in verses twenty two to thirty one:

> *"And straightway Jesus constrained his disciples to get into a ship, and to go before him unto the other side, while he sent the multitude away. And when he had sent the multitude away, he went up into a mountain apart to pray: and when the evening was come, he was there alone"* (22-23).

I will pause here to say, Jesus had just been thronged with a crowd of people whom He had just performed a miracle of feeding the five thousand with two fishes and five loaves. He wanted to get alone with the Father to pray and communicate with Him. So up the mountain he climbs until he reaches a spot that gives Him the serenity he needs, plus provide a vantage point of where He can keep His eye on His disciples out on the open water. We now pick up our text in verse 24 and following:

"But the ship was now in the midst of the sea, tossed with waves: for the wind was contrary. And in the fourth watch of the night (the Romans divided the night into four watches: and the fourth watch was between 3am and 6am) Jesus went unto them, walking on the sea. And when the disciples saw him walking on the sea, they were troubled, saying, It is a spirit; and they cried out for fear" (24-26).

Notice, these seasoned fishermen become overwrought with the wind and the waves, as they make little progress across the water because of the contrary wind; their arms are tired from rowing, their backs are sore from bending, their emotions are raw from the raging sea. And, on top of all this they see a ghostly figure crossing the water walking atop the rolling waves as it slowly approaches them and it unnerves them even more for they cry out like little girls!

> *"But straightway Jesus spake unto them, saying, Be of good cheer; it is I: be not afraid. And Peter answered him and said, Lord, if it be thou, bid me come unto thee on the water"* (27-28).

While the other disciples are quite content to stay in the safety of the boat, Peter the bold fisherman, gets a moment of inspiration that he wants to join his Master on the waves! But where the rubber meets the road and where Peter's feet meet the waves is when he exercises that faith of his to go out and meet Jesus, while risking his life and limbs in the process!

I can just imagine the smile on Jesus' face as He sees the faith of His disciple who wants to join Him atop the water! And Jesus gives Peter a invitation he cannot deny!

> *"And he said, Come. And when Peter was come down out of the ship, he walked on the water to go to Jesus"* (29).

Most ministers when preaching this passage place all the emphasis on Peter's lack of faith in taking his eyes off of Jesus and sinking. But I feel they hold the wrong end of the most important aspect of this text. And that is PETER'S FAITH. Yes, it wasn't what it needed to be to stay atop the water. His faith was still growing. But, and this is a big "but", Peter did possess the right AMOUNT OF FAITH to get out of the boat in the first place and step on down atop what could have been a watery grave! This is the only account in the history of the world where a mortal man actually walked on the water with Jesus! Jesus was the One providing the supernatural ability to Peter in concert with his faith. I believe we can do anything with a big dynamite God enabling us! We just need faith!

Our Faith Lesson today is stepping out on faith and this is a real example of a follower of Christ stepping out on faith, even for a brief while. Let us continue with the rest of our passage:

"But when he saw the wind boisterous, he was afraid; and

beginning to sink, he cried, saying, Lord, save me. And immediately Jesus stretched forth his hand, and caught him, and said unto him, O thou of little faith, wherefore didst thou doubt" (30-31)?

I believe the tone in Jesus' voice was not one of chastisement and correction; but one of acknowledgement and encouragement! Peter had possessed the faith to step out of the boat and onto the storm-tossed waves; he was willing to risk his neck for God and he demonstrated that faith by his actions! Peter got a taste of the supernatural that night! And once you get a taste of the supernatural you don't want to stay in the safety of the boat! You want to do "big things" for a big God!

CHAPTER THREE
SEEKING FAITH:

FOUR DAYS ON THE MOUNTAIN

"What is my life that I should keep it selfishly for me?

I choose to lose it so completely and have it found in Thee."

E. A. Johnston

FAITH LESSON: Seeking Faith: Four Days on the Mountain

BIBLE PASSAGE: Colossians 1:10

Years ago, after my wife tragically died, I decided to go on a "faith journey". I asked God to increase my faith and to make me a man of faith. I earnestly sought Him in prayer and pouring over His Word to bring me to the place of more faith! God answered that prayer when He showed me four truths out of His Word from Colossians 1:10.

At the time, I was rising at 4:30am to have my daily quiet time with God, in prayer and Bible study. One particular morning before dawn, the Lord drew me to Colossians 1:10. He said there were four truths He wanted to teach me out of that verse of Scripture. Truths FROM HIS PERSPECTIVE. He had me read Colossians 1:10 over and over and to give my opinion on it as to what I thought it God meant it to mean to me.

> *"That ye might walk worthy of the Lord unto all pleasing, being fruitful in every good work, and increasing in the knowledge of God"* *(Colossians 1:10).*

And I wrote down in the margin of my Bible what I thought it said to me: *"all pleasing"* means daily obedience and faithfulness under His Lordship. *"Being fruitful"* means abiding in the Vine in a life of yieldedness and surrender to Him. *"and increasing"* means a more intimate knowledge of God in my daily walk with Him. Those were my thoughts that I wrote down that morning. God told me that if I would give Him the next four mornings from 4:30am to 6am, He would reveal to me what that verse meant to me FROM HIS

PERSPECTIVE. He would break it down into four main truths over the course of four days: one for each day. I was getting ready to have my mountaintop experience with a "Dynamite God!" That week was so special to me that I always refer to that time as

"FOUR DAYS ON THE MOUNTAIN"

DAY ONE ON THE MOUNTAIN:

August 15th, 2013, 4:30am to 6am: *"That ye might walk worthy of the Lord."* God would always give me a companion verse to go along with the truth for today. He said my counterpart verse for *"That ye might walk worthy of the Lord"* was to be found in Philippians 3:10:

> *"That I may know him, and the power of his resurrection, and the fellowship of his sufferings, being made conformable unto his death."*

God said my companion verse was to be FROM HIS PERSEPECTIVE: *"walk worthy in the fellowship of MY sufferings."*

Little did I realize at the time the trials, and afflictions I would pass through over the next several years. But that was the truth God wanted me to gain from my first day on the mountain with Him. For to me to *"walk worthy of the Lord"* I would have to experience the *"fellowship of His sufferings."*

Plural. God told the Apostle Paul through His messenger Ananias,

> *"For I will shew him how great things (plural) he must suffer for my name's sake"* (Acts 9:16).

DAY TWO ON THE MOUNTAIN:

August 16th, 2013, 4:30am to 6am: *"unto all pleasing."* In my quiet time this particular morning God gave me His companion verse from HIS PERSPECTIVE of Hebrews 11:6:

> *"But without faith it is impossible to please him."*

And God said that the truth for me this morning regarding my faith walk was: that He would develop a faith life in me that was deep and real. And God would give me plenty of opportunities over the next few years to develop this life of faith to be more pleasing to Him for His glory! And the FAITH LESSON HERE was in the last part of Hebrews 11:6:

> *"…he is a rewarder of them that diligently seek him."*

And this was the answer to my seeking of more faith each morning as I met with the Lord. And this is true for any believer in Christ Jesus, that if we get serious with God, He will get serious with us!

DAY THREE ON THE MOUNTAIN:

August 17th, 2013, 4:30am to 6am: *"being fruitful in every good work."* The companion verse God gave me from HIS PERSPECTIVE was Zechariah 4:6:

> *"This is the word of the LORD unto Zerubbabel, saying, Not by might, nor by power, but by my Spirit, saith the LORD of hosts."*

God said: "My Spirit must be in control at all times through your surrendered life."

God was to make me His empty and clear channel through which He could flow through by His power as a means of a blessing to others. That through my service to Him, fruit was not something I was to produce through fleshly effort and human enterprise; I was not to be a "fruit producer" but to merely be a "fruit bearer" of His Spirit's activity in and through my life. This was the fruit that would last for eternity! The main FAITH LESSON HERE is: it is not so much what we do for Him that counts; but what He does through us that lasts! A self-reliant church that operates on money and manpower is a mere human institution, much like a business corporation. The church should operate on prayer and Holy Ghost power!

DAY FOUR ON THE MOUNTAIN:

August 18th, 2013, 4:30am to 6am: *"and increasing in the knowledge of God."* The companion verse God gave me for this day from HIS PERSPECTIVE was Jeremiah 33:3:

> *"Call unto me and I will answer thee, and shew thee*

great and mighty things, which thou knowest not."

God said: "You will experience more of Me, through the fulfilled promises I have revealed to Thee." And God gave me 18 promises from Isaiah each beginning with verse 18 of each given passage of Scripture promises.

That through each of these things God would build faith in me. that I would become a man of faith. Ten years later this has all been so true! I have had my faith tested, tried, stretched, examined, to where I can truly say I do have a deeper life of faith today in answer to mountaintop experience with God over those four days, which He worked out in a practical way in me through the next ten years. We must have a priority of seeking God in a deeper way, and by going deeper with God we will experience more of God that will transform us into Christ's likeness more and more as we serve God in our generation for His glory!

CHAPTER FOUR
ENCOUNTERING GOD

"When Jesus was here in His earthly ministry, as He passed through towns and villages, those who encountered Him experienced change."

E. A. Johnston

FAITH LESSON: Encountering God

BIBLE PASSAGE: Exodus 3:1-6

In the Book of Exodus, we read of Moses having an encounter with God in the desert, as God speaks to Moses out of a burning bush.

"Now Moses kept the flock of Jethro his father in law, the priest of Midan: and he led the flock to the backside of the desert, and came to the mountain of God, even to Horeb. And the angel of the LORD appeared unto him in a flame of fire out of the midst of a bush: and he looked, and, behold, the bush

burned with fire, and the bush was not consumed. And Moses said, I will now turn aside, and see this great sight, why the bush is not burnt. And when the LORD saw that he turned aside to see, God called unto him out of the midst of the bush, and said, Moses, Moses. And he said, Here am I. And he said, Draw not nigh hither: put off thy shoes from off thy feet, for the place whereon thy standest is holy ground. Moreover he said, I am the God of thy father, the God of Abraham, the God of Isaac, and the God of Jacob. And Moses hid his face; for he was afraid to look upon God" (Exodus 3:1-6).

From this encounter with God much can be derived upon closer examination. First, Moses had to have been in a place of receptivity to this encounter for it to have the intended effect upon him. Notice God waited to speak to Moses until He noticed that Moses had turned out of the way of his path of sheepherding to walk over towards the spectacular sight of the burning bush. God wanted to be assured He had Moses' complete attention. Secondly, Moses had to have been in place of spiritual desperation before this encounter could occur. We notice the following observations of F. J. Huegel:

> "For forty years on the lonely slopes of Midian the fiery Moses is schooled. There were graves, if I may so speak, scattered all over the mountainside where hope after hope was buried until at last self went down in utter annihilation."

So Moses was in a place of spiritual brokenness and hungry for this encounter with a holy God. This encounter with God at the burning bush radically transformed him and altered the entire course of his life. We see from the following:

Moses lived to be 120 years old. The first 40 years of Moses' life in Egypt is covered by 15 verses of Scripture (Exodus 2:1-15). The next 40 years of Moses' life, on the backside of the Midian desert, is covered by only 10 verses of Scripture (Exodus 2:15-25). But the record of Moses' life AFTER HE ENCOUNTERED GOD is covered by approximately 4,252 verses of Scripture! Surely, this clearly demonstrates the significance of a life lived for God after that person has an encounter with God.

Duncan Campbell was remarkably used of God in the Lewis Revival of 1949-1952 in the Scottish Hebrides, where a powerful revival gripped the island to such a degree, it was said that

> "the entire island was saturated
> with the consciousness of God."

I knew a minister on the Isle of Lewis who knew Duncan Campbell well, and I asked him one time to describe to me Duncan Campbell in one sentence: he said,

> "Duncan Campbell was an
> ordinary man who had had an
> extraordinary experience of
> God."

Our Faith Lesson today is on the subject of encountering God. Having an encounter with God is different from God's

Spirit speaking to us in His written word. We read in 1 Kings:

> *"And the word of the LORD came to Solomon, saying"* (1 Kings 6:11).

This occurs when a believer is reading God's Word and through that passage or verse of Scripture the Holy Spirit will apply it to the heart and make it real in the life. But we read of a different nature of this in 1 Kings chapter nine: *"That the LORD appeared to Solomon the second time, as he had appeared unto him at Gibeon"* (1 Kings 9:2). This is altogether different from the other.

A NEEDED ENCOUNTER

Let me share my own personal experience regarding this distinction. Years ago I was literally working myself into the grave. I was working 16-18 hours a day, maintaining a full time secular job and, at the same time, writing and researching my 1,200 page definitive biography on George Whitefield. I had been retracing Whitefield's footsteps throughout Great Britain and America. plus maintaining a family, and a ministry, and I was plumb worn out. One evening I awoke about 2am with a pressure on my chest, I thought I was having a heart attack. I sat up in bed and got up and went across the hall to my study where I plopped down at my desk before my open Bible.

I was ready to die and go to heaven. The work load upon me was just too much. As I sat there before my Bible I prayed to the Lord and I said to God: "Lord, I'm ready to come home to You. I'm worn out. I am ready right now to come home to You--if You will have me. Will You come for me now?"

And right there and then I had an encounter with God. It was as if God was sitting right next to me and He was speaking to me face to face. He asked me a question. Jesus in the Gospels often answered a question with a question. And He asked me a question:

"What do you do for a living?"

"Investments," I answered.

"I have an investment in you, and I will receive the dividends from My investment."

Case closed. The encounter served its purpose and I went back to bed. And I went back to serving Him without complaining. By the way, He has been receiving His dividends from me for these last 18 years.

CHAPTER FIVE
FAITH FOR TRAGEDY

"I had to go downstairs and tell my fourteen-year-old daughter that her mother had just killed herself."

E. A. Johnston

FAITH LESSON: Faith for Tragedy

BIBLE PASSAGE: Job 1:1-22

"And there was a day when his sons and his daughters were eating and drinking wine in their eldest brother's house: and there came a messenger unto Job, and said, The oxen were plowing, and the asses feeding besides them: And the Sabeans fell upon them, and took them away; yea, they have slain the servants with the edge of the sword: and I only am escaped alone to tell thee. While he was yet speaking, there came also another, and said, The fire of God is fallen from heaven, and

hath burned up the sheep, and the servants, and consumed them: and I only am escaped alone to tell thee. While he was yet speaking, there came also another, and said, The Chaldeans made out three bands, and fell upon the camels, and have carried them away, yea, and slain the servants with the edge of the sword: and I only am escaped alone to tell thee. While he was yet speaking, there came also another, and said, Thy sons and thy daughters were eating and drinking wine in their eldest brother's house: And behold, there came a great wind from the wilderness, and smote the four corners of the house, and it fell upon the young men, and they are dead: and I only am escaped alone to tell thee. Then Job arose, and rent his mantle, and shaved his head, and fell down upon the ground, and worshiped. And said, Naked came I out of my mother's womb, and naked shall I return thither: the LORD gave, and the LORD hath taken away: blessed be the name of the LORD. In all this Job sinned not, nor charged God foolishly" (Job 1: 13-22).

My teenage daughter and I had just returned from an early morning walk in the park. As we arrived home, she went to her room to change and I went upstairs to my room to do the same. What I found there was my wife's body—she had taken her own life. Words cannot express the shock, terror, grief that ensued for both of us! It was a horrible unforeseen tragedy. It was like having my own personal 911, I had to handle the situation and go downstairs and tell my fourteen-year-old daughter that her mother had just killed herself. We just held each other crying and crying. Little did I know that at the police station I would be treated like the number one suspect in my wife's murder. The lead detective interrogated me, dusted my hands for gunpowder residue, took a swab of a barbeque stain that was on my pant leg.

And he treated me like I was guilty, guilty, guilty. And he treated me that way all the way up to the autopsy—which proved my wife took her own life.

On top of all this chaos, while I was waiting for the detective to interrogate me again, I was forced to sit next to a tv set in the waiting room that was on loud volume, and the tv talk show host was discussing graphic sex acts and perversion. I couldn't believe it! I cupped my hands over my ears to drown out the profane tv show and it was as it I had a visitor show up next to me. To my dying day I will believe that His Satanic Majesty came to that police station that day to mock me. A noticeable dark presence was MOCKING ME. All Hell was coming against me on that day! I realized I was now a single parent with a traumatized teenage daughter that I had to be both Father and Mother and I had to be sure she attended grief counseling and made progress in emotional healing, before I could even think about taking care of me.

When we lose a loved one unexpectedly it is common to charge God and question Him. Some people get mad at God for removing their loved one from them. Some people lose their religion. Some people lose their faith. But, in Job's case, as should be true with every believer, "Job sinned not, nor charged God foolishly."

How do you prepare for personal tragedy? You don't. Life comes at you at times unexpectedly and suddenly with terrible news. How do you get through something horrible like that? Faith got me through. I will never be able to understand how a lost person gets through a personal tragedy without Jesus Christ. One doesn't get faith in a personal trial or tragedy; you have to have it before the event occurs. It is "having faith" that gets you through the trauma, the grief, the tragedy.

Our Faith Lesson today is important because we need faith not only to grow in our Christian walk with God, we need faith to serve God in deeper ways and in wider opportunities for service, we need faith for the bad times; we need faith to hang onto God when times get tough—too tough for us to deal with it on our own.

CHAPTER SIX
THE DAILY QUIET TIME

"One's prayer life is developed daily over time: it is not built under pleasant sunny skies but beneath dark storm-tossed nights; where faith hangs on a tattered thread and all hope seems gone like the passing wind—and only a God-sent miracle can rescue you."

E. A. Johnston

FAITH LESSON: The Daily Quiet Time

BIBLE PASSAGE: Mark 1:35

We read in Mark's Gospel in chapter one:

"And in the morning, rising up a great while before day, he went out and departed into a solitary place, and there prayed" (Mark 1:35).

If Jesus, as the Son of God, needed to get alone with the Father each day for times

43

of prayer, how much more do we? My homiletical mentor, Dr. Stephen F. Olford taught me the necessity of the Daily Quiet Time. He wrote a little booklet on that subject entitled, "Manna In The Morning" and it is worth its weight in gold! Our devotional life is our spiritual thermometer that gauges our walk with God—either cold or hot! We find in 1 Samuel 2:1, three power-packed words:

"And Hannah prayed."

The desperate prayer of that barren woman touched the very heart of God in heaven. Desperate prayer has wings, a force, a power!

I had had a busy week where I was at a preaching conference, and each day began at 4:30am and I didn't fall into bed until midnight. The conference ended on a Thursday. I was exhausted. The next morning I rushed my daily quiet time because I was running late for my office. What a mistake that was! During the day I sinned. And on the drive home I was talking to God: "Lord, how could I have sinned like that! Especially, after a week long preaching conference! How could I have sinned so easily as that!" I kept asking Him on that long drive home. And a passage of Scripture was brought to my mind: out of Exodus chapter sixteen. About the Israelites and the manna. How God provided the manna each day for their daily nourishment and sustenance. And they were ordered by Moses not to hoard the manna, for what would happen if they hoarded it? It bred worms and stank!

And as I was thinking about that passage of Scripture and the manna, a voice spoke to me: "Like the manna, you must come to Me afresh every morning to have a fresh experience of Me. For you CANNOT LIVE ON YESTERDAY'S EXPERIENCE OF ME. YOU MUST MEET ME FRESH EVERY DAY!"

The reason why I had stumbled and sinned, was because I was relying on yesterday's experience of Him. The importance of the Daily Quiet Time cannot be overstated. Our Faith Lesson today is to develop a daily devotional time with our Lord. To grow in the grace and knowledge of Him. And to have our faith strengthened, stretched, and enlarged. Dr. Olford used to say to me: "We are only as tall in the pulpit, as we are long on our knees!" Make time to pray. Take time to pray. You will be glad you did!

CHAPTER SEVEN
FAITH TESTED

"Faith is looking through the visible to see the invisible to grab the impossible."

E. A. Johnston

FAITH LESSON: Faith Tested

BIBLE PASSAGE: Genesis chapter 22

I once asked God to make me a man of faith. I was determined to become a man of faith. Through the years through many trials and testing, God has developed my faith. When Jesus was here in His earthly ministry, He spent a great deal of time "building faith" in His disciples. He would challenge them with the words, *"O ye of little faith."* Or "Where is your faith?" He was quick to commend faith found in others like the Gentile woman and the Centurion.

God will place us in places and circumstances that are more conducive to building our faith. Often, these circumstances come in times of trial, affliction, and adversity. But one thing is for certain—our faith will be tested so it can grow.

Although our passage of Scripture today is a familiar one, about Abraham sacrificing Isaac, it is a lesson we need to pay close attention to in order for our faith to grow as well. We pick up the narrative in verse four and following of chapter twenty two of Genesis. God has already ordered Abraham to give his son Isaac to God for a burnt offering. We see Abraham's obedience in the following:

"Then on the third day Abraham lifted up his eyes, and saw the place afar off. And Abraham said unto his young men, Abide ye here with the ass; and I and the lad will go yonder and worship, and come again to you. And Abraham took the wood of the burnt offering , and laid it upon Isaac his son; and he took the fire in his hand, and a knife: and they went both of them together. And Isaac spake unto Abraham his father, and said, My

father: Here am I, my son. And he said, Behold the fire and the wood: but where is the lamb for a burnt offering? And Abraham said, My son, God will provide himself a lamb for a burnt offering: so they went both of them together. And they came to the place which God had told him of; and Abraham built an altar there, and laid the wood in order, and bound Isaac his son, and laid him on the altar upon the wood. And Abraham stretched forth his hand, and took the knife to slay his son.

"And the angel of the LORD called unto him out of heaven, and said, Abraham, Abraham; and he said, Here am I. And he said, Lay not thine hand upon the lad, neither do thou anything unto him; for thou I know that thou fearest God, seeing thou hast not withheld thy son, thine only son from me" (Genesis 22: 4-12).

God will place us in trying circumstances as well to test our faith. To see if it is real. I will never forget the story of Manley Beasley traveling to Mexico to visit with F. J. Huegel, because Manley had read Heguel's *"Bone of His Bone"* and it made an impression upon him. And Manley wanted to meet F. J. Huegel to see if what he wrote was REAL IN HIS LIFE.

God wants our faith to be real in our life. Therefore, He will give us plenty of opportunities to stretch our faith, strengthen our faith, and to develop our faith into a more reliable stronger faith! Our Faith Lesson today is that faith will be tested. Has He tested yours lately?

CHAPTER EIGHT
MEN OF FAITH

"The Hall of Faith in Hebrews chapter eleven shames me every time I read it."

E. A. Johnston

FAITH LESSON: Men of Faith

BIBLE PASSAGE: Hebrews 11:1-40

I have known some men of faith whose lives for Christ have challenged me. Two men stand out in particular: Adrian Rogers and Stephen Olford. Both of these men of faith challenged me to live more fully for God and eternity. Adrian Rogers was my pastor at Bellevue Baptist Church in Memphis, Tennessee. Adrian Rogers made me think of Jesus. Every time I was with him he made me more thirsty for Jesus. Have you known someone like that? That every time you were with that person they were so full of Christ that they made you more thirsty for Christ? Adrian was like that. Let me give you an example of how this man of faith impacted me.

It was a rainy night in Memphis, and I had just dropped off my family at the door of the restaurant while I went to park the car. I made my way quickly beneath my umbrella in the dark parking lot in the pouring rain. Finally, upon reaching the door I opened it and there in the lobby was the lone figure of a man with light all around him. He had his arms outstretched and upon seeing me he exclaimed, "Ernesto!" (Adrian Rogers called me Ernesto) and he wrapped his big arms around me in a bear hug of affection. It was Adrian Rogers and as he was hugging me I felt as if I had left this orb and was standing in heaven with Jesus greeting me—that's how it felt. Adrian made me think of Jesus.

Another man, my homiletical mentor, Dr. Stephen F. Olford had a profound influence upon my life. Dr. Olford was a man of faith and a holy man of God. I will illustrate this with the following story about Stephen Olford:

A Dallas pastor had invited Dr. Olford to come preach at his church. The pastor called a seminary intern into his office to give him the following instructions. He said,

"I want you to go to the airport and pick up Dr. Olford who is arriving this afternoon on a flight from Memphis. Here is the gate number."

The young intern inquired: "How will I recognize him? Do you have a photo of him?"

The pastor replied: "No need for that. Just go to the airport terminal and as the passengers deplane, look for a man who has GOD ALL OVER HIM."

Sure enough, as the seminary intern watched the passengers come down the corridor he spotted a man with his coat over his arm and a brief case in his hand—and this man HAD GOD ALL OVER HIM. That story always reminds me of the prophet Elisha and the Shulamite woman.

> *"And she said unto her husband, Behold, now, I perceive that this is a holy man of God, which passeth by us continually"* (2 Kings 4:9).

Do you know a holy man of God like that? A man of faith who is so on fire for God that others take notice? I was with Dr. Olford in his study one day and he came looking fatigued and he sunk into his chair, exclaiming, "Excuse me brother, excuse me, while I regather myself! I just finished preaching and virtue has left me." immediately I thought of the passage of Scripture where Jesus is in the midst of a crowd and the woman with the issue of blood touches the hem of His garment, and He exclaims:

> *"Who touched me? When all denied, Peter and they that were with him said, Master, the multitude throng thee and press thee, and sayest thou, Who touched me? And Jesus said, Somebody hath touched me: for I perceive that virtue is gone out of me"* (Luke 9: 45-46).

Stephen Olford was so full of the Holy Ghost from an anointing of the Spirit that when he preached, virtue left him! Can that be said of you, brother pastor?

In Hebrews chapter eleven we encounter a "hall of faith" of worthies. These individuals of faith stand out in black ink on white paper with remarkable testimonies of faith! This chapter truly contains examples of "faith in action"! Let us take the time to soak up all the wonderful examples of men and women of faith who are mentioned here: we will pick up their exemplary lives in verse three:

> *"By faith Abel offered unto God a more excellent sacrifice than Cain, by which he obtained witness that he was righteous, God testifying of his gifts: and by it he being dead yet speaketh. By faith Enoch was translated that he should not see death; and was not found, because God had translated him: for before his translation he had this testimony, that he pleased God.*

> *"But without faith it is impossible to please him: for he that cometh to God must believe that he is, and that he is a rewarder of them that diligently seek him. By faith Noah, being*

warned of God of things not seen as yet, moved with fear, prepared an ark to the saving of his house; by the which he condemned the world, and became heir of the righteousness which is by faith.

"By faith Abraham, when he was called to go out into a place which he should after receive for an inheritance, obeyed; and he went out not knowing whither he went. By faith he sojourned in the land of promise, as in a strange country, dwelling in tabernacles with Isaac and Jacob, the heirs with him of the same promise. For he looked for a city which hath foundations, whose builder and maker is God.

"Through faith also Sarah herself received strength to conceive seed, and was delivered of a child when she was past age, because she judged him faithful who had promised. Therefore sprang there even of

one and him as good as dead, so many as the stars of the sky in multitude, and as the sand which is by the sea shore innumerable.

"These all died in faith, not having received the promises, but having seen them afar off, and were persuaded of them, and embraced them, and confessed that they were strangers and pilgrims on the earth. For they that say such things declare plainly that they seek a country. And truly, if they had been mindful of that country from whence they came out, they might have had opportunity to have returned. But now they desire a better country, that is, a heavenly: wherefore God is not ashamed to be called their God: for he hath prepared them a city.

"By faith Abraham, when he was tried, offered up Isaac: and he that had received the promises offered up his only begotten son. Of whom it was said, That in Isaac shall thy seed be called: Accounting that God was able to raise him up, even from the dead: from whence also he received him in a figure.

"By faith Isaac blessed Jacob and Esau concerning things to come. By faith Jacob, when he was a dying, blessed both the sons of Joseph; and worshipped, leaning upon the top of his staff. By faith Joseph, when he died, made mention of the departing of the children of Israel; and gave commandment concerning his bones.

"By faith Moses, when he was born, was hid three months of his parents, because they saw he was a proper child; and they were not afraid of the king's commandment. By faith Moses, when he was come to years, refused to be called the son of Pharoah's daughter: Choosing *rather to suffer affliction, with the people of God, than to enjoy the pleasures of sin for a season. Esteeming the reproach of Christ greater riches than the treasure in Egypt: for he had respect unto the recompense of the reward. By faith he forsook Egypt, not fearing the wrath of the king: for he endured, as seeing him who is invisible. Through faith he kept the Passover, and the sprinkling of blood, lest he that destroyed the firstborn should touch them. By faith they passed through the Red sea as by dry land: which the Egyptians attempting to do were drowned.*

"By faith the walls of Jericho fell down, after they were compassed about seven days. By faith the harlot Rahab perished not with them that believed not, when she had received the spies with peace.

"And what shall I more say? for the time would fail me to tell of Gideon, and of Barak, and of Samson, and of Jephthah: of David also, of Samuel, and of the prophets. Who through faith subdued kingdoms, wrought righteousness, obtained promises, stopped the mouths of lions, Quenched the violence of fire, escaped the edge of the sword, out of weakness were made strong, waxed valiant in fight, turned to fight the armies of the aliens. Women received their dead raised to life again: and others were tortured, not accepting deliverance; that they might obtain a better resurrection.

"And others had trial of cruel mockings and scourgings, yea, moreover of bonds and imprisonment: They were stoned, they were sawn asunder, were tempted, were slain of the sword: they wandered about in

sheepskins and goatskins; being destitute, afflicted, tormented. (of whom the world was not worthy;) they wandered in deserts, and in mountains, and in dens and caves of the earth. And these all, having obtained a good report through faith, received not the promise: God having provided some better thing for us, that they without us should not be made perfect" (Hebrews 11:4-40).

It is hard to read Hebrews eleven and not get on fire for God and eternity! What examples these worthies are to us today! How shallow our own service to God pales in comparison to the mark they made on their generation!

The culmination of this laundry list of faith heroes is the mention of them beginning in chapter twelve:

"Wherefore seeing we also are compassed about with so great a cloud of witnesses , let us lay aside every weight, and the sin which doth so easily beset us,

and let us run with patience that is set before us. Looking unto Jesus the author and finisher of our faith; who for the joy that was set before him endured the cross, despising the shame, and is set down at the right hand of the throne of God" (12:1-2).

We see this mention of *"a great cloud of witnesses."* This verse is loaded with a double meaning: that those mentioned in Hebrews chapter eleven in the "Hall of Faith" are EXAMPLES set before us to emulate. They are also, SPECTATORS in our Christian race, filling up a great heavenly amphitheater cheering us on as we run for the prize which is Jesus Christ our Lord! When I was a younger man I visited Olympia, Greece and toured the original stadium of the first Olympics. Two other men in our tour group wanted to have a race, so the three of us took our mark and ran as fast as we could imagining ourselves as the first Greek athletes while the rest of the tour group cheered us on! It was exciting to run where history had taken place so long ago. How much more exciting to run the race for Christ and His Kingdom while we are in this world as followers of His! Men of faith who have gone before us should challenge each of us to examine our own service to God and see how we can improve it and expand it for His glory!

CHAPTER NINE
A SUPER DUPER GOD

"God is the same God today as He was working miracles in the Old and New Testaments. We could see Him move in that same capacity today if we could 'only believe.'"

E. A. Johnston

FAITH LESSON: A SUPER DUPER GOD

BIBLE PASSAGE: Mark 9:23 & 10:27

Remember Vance Havner's comment about God?

"If we serve such a dynamite God, then how come so many of us are living firecracker lives?"

I believe the answer lies in one word: FAITH. Our possession of it or our lack of it. Do we really believe that the God we serve is the same God of Abraham, Isaac, and Jacob? And that He hasn't gone out of the miracle working business? Is our faith like the passage from Ezekiel?

"And when the man that had the line in his hand went forth eastward, he measured a thousand cubits, and he brought me through the waters; the waters were to my ankles. Again he measured a thousand, and brought me through the waters; the waters were to the knees. Again he measured a thousand and brought me through; the waters were to the loins. Afterward he measured a thousand; and it was a river that I could not pass over: for the waters were risen, waters to swim in…" (Ezekiel 47: 3-5).

What this passage speaks to, in regard to our faith, is that some of us only have enough faith to go in to the ankles; others enough faith to go in to our knees; some to possess more faith to wade in up to the loins: while some have enough faith to jump in and swim! We can hinder God's work in our life by our lack of faith. We can restrict God's blessings for us through our lack of faith. We see this reality in Matthew's Gospel:

"And He did not many mighty works there because of their unbelief" (Matthew 13:58).

Do we really believe that our God is a super duper God who can do dynamite things? Or do we believe God went out of the miracle working business because that was just for the New Testament church. He doesn't work like that today. Go get a copy of *"The Journel Once Lost: Diary of John Sung"* written by his daughter Levi, and see how a miracle working God was performing miracles under John Sung's powerful ministry in China during the mid 20th century! The blind received sight. The lame threw down their crutches as they were no longer needed. During one revival a cross appeared in the sky that was witnessed by many! China was literally turned upside down for God in revival and hundreds of thousands were saved under the preaching of evangelist John Sung. John Sung maintained a "big faith" in a "big God". On a blank check he wrote the words: BANK OF

HEAVEN, March 22, 1932, 100,000 souls. (as a request to the Lord). The next year he had to write another check for another request of 100,000 souls, because that one was cashed!

We find a connecting truth in the Gospel of Mark in regard to faith.

> *"And Jesus looking upon them saith, With men it is impossible, but not with God: for with God all things are possible"* (Mark 10:27).

Do we really believe that? If we truly believe that then how come some of us are living "firecracker lives"? We see the connecting verse to Mark 10:27 in Mark 9:23, which declares:

> *"Jesus said unto him, If thou canst believe, all things are possible to him that believeth."*

God made a statement on faith concerning Himself: "with God all things are possible." This is on THE GODWARD SIDE. God made another statement on faith concerning man: "If thou canst believe, all things are possible to him that believeth." This is from THE MANWARD SIDE. Our unbelief not only limits God, it hinders His activity in our lives! Jesus was continually reminding His disciples these truths: "O ye of little faith." "Where is your faith?" More faith—more power. More faith—more dynamite!

Listen to how Jesus describes this very principle of having faith in His interactions with others during His earthly ministry:

"And Jesus said unto the centurion, Go thy way; and as thou hast believed so be it done unto thee. And his servant was healed in the selfsame hour" (Matthew 8:13).

"Then touched he their eyes, saying, According to your faith be it unto you" (Matthew 9:29).

"And their eyes were opened; and Jesus straitly charged them, saying, See that no man know it" (Matthew 9:30).

"And Jesus said unto them, Because of your unbelief: for verily I say unto you, If ye have faith as a grain of mustard seed, ye shall say unto this mountain, Remove hence to yonder place; and it shall remove: and nothing shall be impossible unto you" (Matthew 17:20, 21:21).

If God has placed it on our hearts to pray for revival, and we are faithful to pray regularly for revival; He will take that and add to it and give us a BURDEN FOR REVIVAL. And if we believe in the God of revival, there will come a time when God places us in the midst of revival. Go study revival history and see if this principle is not true. True intercessory prayer labors beneath a burden to see the reality of the answered prayer. If you look behind the record of each historical revival you will find one or more persons who labored in prayer for that revival to come! But there has to be an accompanying belief that God will send revival and revival will come.

God is a super duper God who does dynamite things! And God is a dynamite God who does super duper things! If we only believe.

72

CHAPTER TEN
THE PAIN AND GAIN OF FAITH

"Jonathan Edwards knew the cost of revival. After seeing God move in several seasons of glorious revival, the last fourteen years of Edward's life were filled with trouble, trial, grief, opposition, turmoil, and termination. He had to witness the early death of his young friend, David Brainerd. Four months later he suffered the personal loss of the sudden death of his eighteen-year-old daughter, Jerusha. He was then thrust into a scene of great controversy and opposition in his own church which resulted in his removal. He and his large family were suddenly thrust into privation and cast upon the world with no financial support and he ended up in the wilderness of

Stockbridge, MA with a ministry of preaching to a mere handful of Indians. While laboring there in inclement weather he came down with a severe fever that made him an invalid for a period of seven months, which greatly weakened his already strained constitution. From there he had a brief promotion to the President of the College of New Jersey, only to die before assuming his labors at the age of 54 from a fatal reaction to a new vaccine. He died with the weight of the world upon him as he entered a better world, where pain, suffering, and struggle were no more. By the way, did I mention that these last fourteen years of his life was his greatest period of productivity, whereby he wrote the bulk of his written legacy to the Church at large."

E. A. Johnston

FAITH LESSON: The Pain & Gain of Faith

BIBLE PASSAGE: Job 5:6&7; 17&18

Years ago when I asked God to make me a man of faith I was willing to undergo change for this to occur. Little did I know at the time that the change which would occur would be PAINFUL.

Often as we pass through trial and trouble our friends can misread what is transpiring in our life and point their fingers in accusation and judgment as to why we are in that trial. This certainly was the case with Job's friend Eliphaz, who was wrong in his assumptions of Job's troubles.

Although it is true that sin brings us low; sin brings trouble and sorrows; at times the reason for our affliction can be altogether different from that. In regard to Job's troubles, Eliphaz concludes: "Although affliction cometh not forth of the dust, neither doth trouble spring out of the ground: Yet man is born unto trouble, as the sparks fly upward" (Job 5:6-7). Eliphaz's conclusions regarding Job's sufferings were based on his own opinion and ignorance as to what God was doing in Job's life. Eliphaz was completely unaware that God was permitting this circumstance of suffering in Job's life for a purpose other than his own sinful nature. This trial of Job was permitted for a purifying of Job's faith just as gold is placed in the furnace of affliction to purge away all dross and reduce it to its finest purity. This season of suffering for Job would accomplish God's purpose of strengthening Job's faith.

As in body building there is a slogan: "No pain, no gain." This is true in FAITH BUILDING as well. And we see God's purpose behind Job's suffering in the following verses:

> *"Behold, happy is the man whom God correcteth: therefore despise not thou the chastening of the Almighty: For he maketh sore, and bindeth up: he woundeth, and his hands make whole"* (Job 5:17-18).

Whether we are being chastised for sin in our life, with God's purpose of correcting us to turn in repentance and a forsaking of that sin altogether; or we are under the chastisement of the Almighty for His hidden purposes of purifying and strengthening our faith, we should submit to the Refiner's Fire and the will of God in our life.

At times like this, our prayer to God should be:

"LORD, I ALIGN MYSELF TO THEE AND THY PURPOSE BENEATH YOUR CHASTISING HAND FOR CORRECTION AND GROWTH IN THAT YOUR WORK WILL BE DONE IN ME TO PURIFY AND STRENGTHEN MY FAITH."

When Jonathan Edwards was passing through his greatest trials, God was building faith in him for further usefulness and to be made more conformable to the image of Christ Jesus.

Our Faith Lesson is the Pain and Gain of faith. We conclude with the following verses of Scripture:

"Who in the days of his flesh, when he had offered up prayers and supplications with

strong crying and tears unto him that was able to save him from death, and was heard in that he feared; Though he were a Son, yet learned he obedience by the things which he suffered: And being made perfect, he became the author of eternal salvation unto all them that obey him" (Hebrews 5:7-9).

CHAPTER ELEVEN
THE SACRIFICE OF FAITH

"He said, 'If I am to use you like few other men, then you will have to live like few men do.' This was the final battleground between self and the cross. It was either future usefulness for God or a life of uselessness for me. Self had to be willingly annihilated daily on the cross and there had to be a 'full surrender' to His Lordship in consecration from that point forward, until He came or called—there was no turning back."

E. A. Johnston

FAITH LESSON: The Sacrifice of Faith

BIBLE PASSAGE: 1 John 4:9-10

Anything worthwhile in life has a cost, a sacrifice. Whether it is higher education or learning a trade or sport. If you desire excellence, then there will be a sacrifice of time to study and practice to become good at something. What costs counts and what counts costs.

In the spiritual life this principle applies as well. If you want to master the word of God then you must devote years of diligent study to gain that knowledge. If you want a deeper walk with God then there must be commitment, a sacrifice of time, a consecrated life, a pursuit of holiness. We see that God delights in sacrifice as seen in His written word from 1 John:

> *"In this was manifested the love of God toward us, because that God sent his only begotten Son into the world, that we might live through him. Herein is love, not that we loved God, but that he loved us, and sent his Son to be the propitiation for our sins"* (1 John 4:9-10).

Years ago, I wanted to get serious with God and I was challenged by the following story while re-reading David Wilkerson's book, *"The Cross and the Switchblade"*, I was impressed by a facet in Wilkerson's life. Early in his ministry he was a country pastor who spent the hours of midnight to 2am watching television to unwind and relax. One evening God challenged Wilkerson to give that time to Him. Wilkerson sold his TV and never replaced it. From that point forward he gave God midnight to 2am, and it was during this time that God called Wilkerson to NYC to minister among teen gang members, eventually starting Teen Challenge. I realized that God did not reveal this wider ministry opportunity to Wilkerson until he chose to go deeper with God in a sacrificial daily quiet time, in his case, from midnight to 2am which was devoted to prayer and Bible study, and seeking the Lord's will for his life.

I had maintained a daily, regular quiet time for many years, but lately my time with the Lord was missing something—there was no SACRIFICE attending it. And the God of the Bible delights in sacrifice, for He sacrificed His only begotten Son for sinful man. After reading Wilkerson's story, I made a covenant with God to rise at 4:30am and give God the first hour and a half of each day—walking with Him. It is amazing how God honored that time! It was around this time that God challenged me to become a man of faith. God gets serious with those who get serious with Him. Let me ask you a question and please be honest. Does your daily quiet time with God have a sacrificial aroma attending it? Is your sweetheart love for Christ more passionate today than yesterday? His desire is to SPEND TIME WITH YOU. God is looking for the one who will walk closely with Him. Those Enochs will be translated to a deeper walk and wider usefulness to Him for His glory!

CHAPTER TWELVE
FAITH AND CROOKED THINGS

"If God reveals to us an area of our life that is out of step with Him, how can we progress in our faith life without straightening out this crooked thing? Does not Amos 3:3 declare: *'Can two walk together, except they be agreed?'*"

E. A. Johnston

FAITH LESSON: Faith and Crooked Things

BIBLE PASSAGE: Isaiah 42:16

Growing in the grace and knowledge of God is a process of sanctification that never really stops until we get to heaven. For those believers who want to go deeper with God in their faith life the challenges will be many—but worthwhile.

In Isaiah chapter forty two and in verse sixteen, we find our teaching point for today's lesson. Our Faith Lesson for today is straightening out the crooked things in our life that hinder our walk with God and restrict our usefulness to Him. In God's word we read:

> *"And I will bring the blind by a way that they knew not; I will lead them in paths that they have not known: I will make darkness light before them, and crooked things straight. These things will I do unto them, and not forsake them"* (Isaiah 42:16).

The best way to illustrate this principal to us in this Faith Lesson of putting crooked things straight, is to relate to you a story that has had a profound impact on me. Here now is that story:

In the 1930's a Presbyterian pastor by the name of Ernest Wadsworth experienced a personal revival that eventually became a localize revival that turned his church and community upside down. He wrote a book about it entitled, "Will Revival Come?" And it was one of the most stirring accounts I ever read on how God dealt with a man's faith and challenged the faith of others. This is his story:

He was to attend an annual state meeting for his denomination which was to have five hundred of his fellow ministers there. But previous to the date of the conference the five hundred pastors were asked to fill out a questionnaire on the chief reason for the hindrance to seeing revival in their churches. Now remember this is back in the 1930's when America was still a Christian nation and God was still moving in the churches in the land. This Presbyterian pastor, Ernest Wadsworth filled out his questionnaire and listed what he felt was the main hindrance to seeing revival in the church.

After deep heart searching, he determined that the hindrance was not on God's side but on man's side—particularly the ministers of the church. While at the pastor's state conference the Chairman of evangelism gave a digest of the opinions of the ministers gathered from their questionnaire. About sixty percent expressed a belief that the chief hindrance to revival was due to the non-cooperative spirit of the church officers. Twenty percent believed the chief difficulty in promoting revival was due to the indifference of the members of the churches. Some thought the hindrance to promoting revival was due to the worldly programs or finances. After the Chairman of the evangelistic committee had read the digest of the answers from the questionnaires, he said he had one letter different from all the rest which he wanted them all to hear.

"This letter," said the Chairman, "declares that the blame rests on the ministry itself as the greatest hindrance to revival."

When those five hundred pastors heard that, it produced a long outburst of laughter that shook the building, as these pastors grabbed their bellies and rocked back and forth in their seats howling with laughter.

But this man Wadsworth thought the truth should have produced solemnity and tears of repentance from the pastors, but the opposite occurred—they laughed at such a ridiculous notion! Before attending the conference, Ernest Wadsworth had taken seriously the questionnaire and the hindrance to revival. He attached to the letter his own personal spiritual journey from this experience. After deep self-examination and humiliation before God, he was led into a fresh consecration and devotion to Christ. He found a new power accompanied his ministry and conversions began to occur in the congregation. God's presence was with Joseph and Moses and with the Apostles. And the letter finished with plea to his fellow ministers there to re-consecrate themselves to the Lord to be channels of blessings that God could flow through. When the meeting was over this man Wadsworth introduced himself to the Chairman of the committee saying, "Dr. so and so, it was I who wrote that letter." Upon hearing this the Chairman glared at him with disgust and turned on his heel without a word and walked briskly away.

His faith had been challenged by his very own denomination! And he was judged unfairly. But this discouragement only strengthened his faith and his determination. He returned home to his church with a burden to see revival, even if he was in the minority. Over the course of the next few months he was called to a new pastorate in a new town, and he prayed and fasted for the right message to preach at his inaugural sermon for his new congregation. He recalled that Charles Spurgeon used to tell his students to pick a text that would make a congregation get up at five o'clock on a frosty morning just to hear it read. Well, this man Wadsworth wanted a text like that, and God finally gave it to him from Isaiah 42:16 about *"Make the Crooked Places Straight."*

This topic so challenged him in his personal life, he felt compelled to write a couple of letters and drop them in the mailbox to make some crooked things straight in his own life before he preached that message to others. He asked himself what is the purpose of this sermon? The purpose of the sermon is to get people to make the crooked things in their life straight so God could have no hindrance to work in their midst so God could prosper. But as he was thinking upon these things God asked him a question: "Have you any crooked things to make straight?" He felt that conviction, and it was as if God said to him: "Unless you straighten these crooked things out, I'll not be with you when you preach your famous sermon tomorrow."

Ernest Wadsworth mailed the two letters and had a good conscience that the crooked things had been made straight. He described what followed:

"I rose early that Sunday morning to have ample time for prayerful preparation. The sermon 'Making Crooked Things Straight' was delivered to a large but restless audience. Some seemed angry, others seemed almost ready to leave their pews. After the benediction, most of the people hurried out as quickly as possible. Upon returning home my dear wife said to me, with a look of reproof, 'You will hear from that sermon but not in the way you expect!' I told her that I believed I faithfully discharged my rights to my duties and I'll leave the results with the Lord.

"That evening, the service was poorly attended. The next morning, I received a call that the mayor wanted me to come to his office. I went to the office of the mayor and was ushered into a private room. After I was seated, the mayor said, 'I heard your sermon yesterday morning. Now, man to man, I want to know whose been telling you about me?' Mister mayor, I preached that sermon to myself and got some things straightened out and I can assure you no one has been gossiping about you to me."

But the mayor did not believe him. The next phone call he got was from the richest man in his congregation, the owner of a department store. He was summoned to this man's office and once he arrived there the man paced the floor nervously with a cigar in his hand. He inquired, "Now Sir, I want to know the names of the people who sent you to preach against me yesterday morning!" I tried to satisfy him that I merely preached the truth that I found in the Word of God, but he didn't believe me. Last of all, the undertaker sent for me late at night and when I arrived at his door, he said he knew my conscience would trouble me for telling his faults to the other members of the congregation.

That month the officials of the church decided to rid themselves of so disturbing a minister and I was fired. Eventually, I was given a new church in the community and from that pulpit the Lord brought a mighty revival that swept through the entire town, to the point that the church could no longer contain the crowds and I had to move our services to the opera house![1]

Well that's the end of his story, but it demonstrates that a man's faith will be tested, even in the fires of persecution, in order to grow that faith and become a clear vessel that God can use to flow through with His revival blessings! Ernest Wadsworth got the crooked things straightened out in his life and he saw incredible blessings in the salvation of souls! It's truly amazing how the power of God can flow through an unobstructed vessel.

After I heard that story I came under conviction myself. I used to work for a man who was a brute. Every time he opened his mouth he damned God and cursed Jesus. It was hard to even be around him for he had such a filthy mouth. He knew I was a Christian and he ended up firing me because he had gotten mad at me over something. But after hearing Ernest Wadsworth's story, I felt I had some crooked

---

[1] Ernest Wadsworth, "Will Revival Come?" (Chicago: Great Commission Prayer, 1936).

things to straighten out myself with some unfinished business with this former boss. I sat down and wrote him a letter. I said, "I want you to know the very Jesus you curse and damn every time you open your mouth hung and suffered on a bloody Cross so you could have forgiveness of sins." I then went on to tell him that every day I worked for him I prayed to God to save him. I asked him to repent and turn to God now before it was too late. I included a Gospel tract with the letter and I went to the post office and mailed it to him.

How about you friend? Is there any unfinished business you need to do to make the crooked things straight?

CHAPTER THIRTEEN
FAITH TRIED

"God builds faith when it is tried. This is done through the Divine process of reducing and decreasing. Gold must be reduced to its purity in the furnace of affliction. A branch must be pruned back with a knife and decreased before it can produce more fruit. If we want our faith to grow in further usefulness to God, then we must submit to both the Refiner's fire and the Divine Pruning knife."

E. A. Johnston

FAITH LESSON: Faith Tried

BIBLE PASSAGE: Psalm 105: 17-21

Our Faith Lesson today is Faith Tried and our object lesson is the life of Joseph. Our main theme in this lesson is poised in a question: "Are we willing to be reduced to nothing so He can be everything through us?"

Joseph was Jacob's favorite son. Perhaps Jacob's affection for Joseph spoiled him but we cannot blame Joseph for that. It was the jealousy toward that favorite son which turned the hearts of his brothers against him. Matthew Henry said of Joseph:

> "First he had to be cast into a pit and a prison before he could be elevated to a prince and ruler."

We read of Joseph's great usefulness and great suffering in Psalm 105:

> *"He sent a man before them, even Joseph, who was sold for a servant. Whose feet they hurt with fetters: he was laid in iron; Until the time that his word came: the word of the LORD tried him. The king sent and loosed him; even the ruler of the people, and let him go free. He made him lord of his house, and ruler of all his substance"* (Psalm 105: 17-21).

"He sent a man before them" refers directly to Genesis 50:20 which states:

"But as for you, ye thought evil against me; but God meant it unto good, to bring to pass, as it is this day, to save much people alive."

The Sovereignty of God works with a Hidden Hand behind the scene of life. In Joseph's case, he would have to endure abandonment and suffering, lose his freedom and his reputation, to sit in iron until God was ready to promote him.

The key word in our FAITH LESSON for today is the word, "tried"; "the word of the LORD tried him." The word "tried" in the Hebrew is an interesting word. It is the word, "Tsaraph" (pronounced "saw raf ") and it means to fuse or refine metal. It speaks of a furnace of fire so hot that a founder, like a goldsmith or silversmith, can refine and test metals. It's a verb meaning to refine or test. And this word describes the purging and purifying process of a refiner who heats metal with the purpose to take away the

97

dross to where what remains is a pure substance of great value. We see this same thought in Proverbs 25:4, *"Take away the dross from the silver, and there shall come forth a vessel for the finer."* This reference is to the Refiner's fire.

And in our text here we have our FAITH LESSON for the day: FAITH TRIED (in the Refiner's fire). When I was in high school, I had a summer job at the local grocery store, and part of my job description was to take the boxes that the produce came in and cut them flat with a box cutter and stack them on a two-wheeler, and then take them to the back of the store where a huge cast iron furnace was. Every time I opened that heavy furnace door I saw the white hot flames swirl and my face would be singed with the awful heat of those flames, as I quickly tossed in those boxes to be burned.

Our Bible passage in Psalm 105 is referring to Joseph in the Refiner's fire. For here is a picture implied of a master tradesman, like a goldsmith or silversmith, intently at work to separate the metal from its impurities; he labors over that heated fire with great concentration and carefulness as he lowers the gold or silver into the flames and holds it there with his iron implement until the gold or silver is purged and refined. But the central thought here is in regard to God's people, in particular, Joseph; for when this word "tried" is applied to God's people it speaks of the purifying effects of external trials that God often uses to build faith and purge sin. It is a painful process that must be take place for God to receive the glory and not man.

We get a further sense of this from God's Word in Isaiah 1:25, where God is describing a sinful nation and His dealings with a rebellious people who need refining. "And I will turn my hand upon thee, and purely purge away thy dross, and take away thy tin." Tin speaks of worthless metal compared to gold. But for gold to have value it must be purged of its dross and impurities.

Our text from Psalm 105 speaks of Joseph in a suffering condition, being tried by outward circumstances beyond his control. He is betrayed by his brethren, cast in a pit, sold for a servant, locked in a prison, held fast in iron. Iron speaks of an ironclad circumstance that no man can extradite himself from: it's a prison of iron. And it is there that Joseph sits until the time that his word came: the word of the LORD tried him." We learn from Genesis 41:1 that Joseph sat in prison a full two years AFTER the baker and the butler were removed from being his prison mates. For we read: "And it came to pass at the end of two full years that Pharoah dreamed: and, behold, he stood by the river" (Genesis 41:1). It was here, in the Refiner's fire, that the work was done to prepare Jospeh for his release and promotion by Pharoah.

Our FAITH LESSON teaches us that as God builds faith in us, as God strengthens our existing faith, as God stretches our faith to make it grow, even though it is often a painful process the end result is worth the trial. Evan Roberts of the Welsh Revival felt his faith tried at the height of the revival. He wrote a poem referring to this time and the last line reads: "Though hellish hosts revile forever I'll lay myself on Christ my Savior!"

One comforting thought from all of this is seen in this fact of the Refiner: When the Silversmith holds the metal under the fire, as it crackles and spits, not once does he ever take his eyes off the silver. God's eyes are upon His saints who are being tried for their faith to grow and to bring glory to Him. We must submit to the Refiner's fire and cooperate with God in His work through us and we must be willing to be reduced to nothing so Jesus can be everything through us!

CHAPTER FOURTEEN
EMPTY OF SELF

"How can a man full of himself, preach the Christ who emptied Himself?"

J. Sidlow Baxter

FAITH LESSON: Empty of Self

BIBLE PASSAGE: Second Samuel 15:30

The Christian life is an impossible life to live in the flesh. The Faith life is never going to reach its fullest potential if self is in the way. Self is a terrible tyrant that demands recognition, seeks advancement and reward, and forces itself to the front of any line to have first place. Ministry is no different from life in the sense that self can get in the way for the busy pastor, traveling evangelist, or seminary professor. We all desire some form of recognition for our efforts—this is only human. There is nothing wrong with recognition for achievements gained—it is wrong when the reason for the achievement was merely recognition.

Our FAITH LESSON today is rich with lessons that we can apply to our own personal faith journey. The world tells us that it is the one with the most toys at the end who is the winner. Christianity tells us not to love the world and live above the world as we prepare for a better world.

Second Samuel chapter fifteen is a striking passage of Scripture. We read in verse thirty:

> *"And David went up by the ascent of mount Olivet, and wept as he went up, and had his head covered, and he went barefoot: and all the people that was with him covered every man his head, and they went up, weeping as they went up"* (Second Samuel 15:30).

Here is a picture of band of desperate people following their exiled leader in utter humiliation. Did you ever try to climb a rocky mountain in your bare feet? Do you know how slashed and bruised and cut and bleeding were David's feet as he ascended mount Olivet, weeping as he climbed. Every step felt like a knife driven into the exposed soles of his feet. David was a warrior who was accustomed to pain; but here is physical pain combined with inward trial. Who is this figure of a man with his head covered weeping as he goes? Is he a homeless person of no report? A beggar perhaps? A criminal on the run? No. He is a king. The King of Israel. You wouldn't know it by looking at this stripped, pitiful figure reduced of self and position. Why is David in this position? His son Absalom was not content to be a king's son—he wants to be king. David is forced from his palace, reduced, and in fear of his life; fleeing with a small band seeking shelter in a desert. And looking over his shoulder to see the city of David which he had built, and now an exile from, is too much for him. His followers see him in distress, but they are few and unable to help him, so they weep beside him.

Sooner or later a believer must tread the way of "empty of self", if further usefulness to God is desired and faith to grow. To go further with God one must come to the end of himself where self must go the way of the Cross. The Cross in the life of a believer is a seldom taught truth in our day of self-promotion and self-help books. Even so-called Christian bookstores have sections devoted to self-help books, promoting the "Best You". But the way of the Cross is lined with the pavement of self-annihilation. Moses had to be schooled in a desert before he could deliver a nation. We see the comments of F. J. Heugel:

> "For forty years on the lonely slopes of Midian the fiery Moses is schooled. There were graves, if I may so speak, scattered all over the mountainside where hope after hope was buried until at last self went down in utter annihilation."

The self-reliant church is a powerless church. The Christian full of self is not living up to his potential in Christ Jesus. This picture in our passage today of a humiliated king should be an object lesson to each of us. There used to be a brass plate on the banister of the pulpit rail of a historic church, and as the preacher would ascend the pulpit stairs his eyes would fall on the writing of the plaque which read: *"Sir, we would see Jesus"* (John 12:21).

CHAPTER FIFTEEN
FAITH AND BROKENNESS

"The word contrite means ground to powder. If you want power with God then be willing to be ground to powder. The two go hand in hand like biscuits and gravy."

E. A. Johnston

FAITH LESSON: Faith and Brokenness

BIBLE PASSAGE: Isaiah 57:15

In the book of Isaiah we read:

"For thus saith the high and lofty One that inhabiteth eternity, whose name is Holy: I dwell in the high and holy place, with him also that is of a contrite and humble spirit, to revive the spirit of the humble, and to revive the heart of the contrite ones" (Isaiah 57:15).

A holy God dwells in a lofty place; a holy God dwells also with the contrite and humble spirit. Our FAITH LESSON today is on brokenness. Going deeper with God means growing deeper in faith. As a tall tree has deep roots beneath the ground that hold it steady in the storms of life, so too the person who has a deepening faith through brokenness will weather any storm.

Brokenness centers around the will. Strong willed individuals will have a tougher time with brokenness. Our Bible passage today is from Isaiah 57:15 and the key word in that text is the word *"contrite."* This verse tells us that although God is a high and lifted One who inhabits eternity and whose name is Holy, He also dwells with the contrite of heart. One who is little in their own eyes. And brokenness here is expressed in that word "contrite" which means to be ground to powder. That is about as low as one can go—to become a pile of powder.

The best way to express this doctrine of brokenness is to illustrate it in a story I once read about the evangelist Sam Jones. it is taken from his biography and it will best explain our lesson for today which is: brokenness. Here now is that story:

Sam Jones was at his home in Cartersville, GA when he received a telegram from Texas inviting him to go to Southwest Texas to preach to the cowboys. After praying about it he boarded a train and traveled to Texas. For two weeks he preached the gospel of Jesus Christ to the cowboys in Texas. When the meetings ended the cowboys wanted to give Sam Jones a love offering. They felt the laborer was worthy of his hire and they had been wonderfully blessed the time Sam had spent among them. But there was a problem—they had no money, not a single dollar in any of their pockets. They didn't know what to do. Sam Jones returned to Cartersville with no love offering or compensation of any kind.

A number of weeks had passed when suddenly one day Sam received a telegram. It was from the cowboys in Texas and it read like this: "We are sending you a love offering and we are shipping you a carload of broncos."

Sam Jones scratched his head as he looked in amazement at that telegram. "What am I gonna do," he said, "with a carload of wild horses in the small town of

Cartersville?" His friend standing beside him said, "Why, it's very easy, hold an auction sale. Sell the horses and you'll get your money. You can get your love offering then and put it in your pocket."

Sam Jones thought it was a good suggestion so when the horses arrived he held a horse auction. He sold the broncos—all except one. He kept the finest looking bronco for his son. But the son had never in his life been on the back of an unbroken bronco and Sam Jones wondered what he could do. He called the cowboy who had brought the carload of broncos to Cartersville and said, "Will you take this bronco and break him so that my son can ride him?"

"Yes, sir," said the cowboy. "I'd be glad to."

"How much will you charge."

"Fifteen dollars," said the cowboy.

"Alright," said Sam, "take him away."

The cowboy disappeared with the bronco. Two weeks later he came back. "Is he broken?" asked Sam.

"Yes, sir, he's broken."

"Can my son ride him in perfect safety?"

"Yes, sir. Your son can ride him in perfect safety."

The father thought that before allowing his son to ride the bronco, he'd better mount himself and make sure the cowboy had broken it. As he started toward the horse, the cowboy came running and waving his hands in alarm. "What's the matter?" asked Sam. "What's gone wrong?"

"Oh," said the cowboy, "he's only broken on one side, and you're mounting from the wrong side."

"That will never do. My son might make a mistake and he might mount from the wrong side. How much will you charge to break him on the other side?"

"Fifteen dollars," replied the cowboy.

"Alright," said Sam. "Take him away and break him on the other side."

Another two weeks passed and again the cowboy came back leading the bronco.

"Is he broken?"

"Yes sir. He's broken."

"Both sides?"

"Yes Sir. Both sides. Your son can ride him in perfect safety from either side."[2]

That story strikes a nerve in our FAITH LESSON for today. You see friend, the average Christian is like that bronco—only broken on one side. He will go here but he won't go there. He'll do this but he won't do that. He's only broken on one side. To grow in the grace and knowledge of Christ Jesus in a life of faith requires that we are broken on BOTH SIDES. It is the contrite ones who are closest to a lofty God whose name is Holy.

---

[2] E. A. Johnston, "Sam Jones A New Biography, (Gainesville: Old Paths Publications) pp 45-48.

CHAPTER SIXTEEN
A DYNAMITE FAITH

"Almighty God has dunamis power which is where we get our word 'dynamite' from. This begs the question: If God is a dynamite God, then why are there so many duds sitting in church on Sunday?"

E. A. Johnston

FAITH LESSON: A Dynamite Faith

BIBLE PASSAGE: 2 Timothy 1:7

In second Timothy we read:

"For God hath not given us the spirit of fear: but of power, and of love, and of a sound mind" (2 Timothy 1:7).

The focus of our FAITH LESSON today is the word, "power" found in this text from 2 Timothy 1:7. The Greek word for power is the word, "dunamis" which is where we get our word "dynamite" from. It is an inherent power in us by His Spirit. It is already at our disposal, we just need to appropriate it by faith and exercise it by obedience.

When we study the lives of Bible characters we see this power in action! Moses had it. Joshua had it. David had it. These were men of faith who had a dynamite life for God that shook their generation. Take a stroll through the Book of Acts and be astounded at this power seen in the lives of Peter and Paul! They stand like titans among mere mortals. Yes, they are beaten; yes, they are imprisoned; yes, they are finally martyred—but their lives for Christ and the Gospel were powder kegs of power that shook their generation for God and eternity! What did they have that we don't have? Why aren't we shaking our community up for God and the Gospel? Because we are gripped with FEAR. Fear of the consequences. We don't want to risk being arrested. We don't want to risk our skin. We are into self-preservation more than going out on a limb for God come hell or high water! But if we stepped out there in faith for God with a mighty witness that did not fear man but only feared the Almighty then all hell would begin to pop!

Let me give you several examples of men of faith whom God has used in powerful ways because they did not fear man and they had a big faith in a big God! In America from 1928 to 1969 an itinerant evangelist by the name of Rolfe Barnard canvassed America with the Gospel of the Son of God. He was not well known to the masses because the churches he preached in were mainly small country churches; but just about everywhere Rolfe Barnard went he would turn a church upside down for God in revival. He preached with a stick of dynamite in one hand and the Bible in the other! There was a noticeable power of God in his meetings that resulted in countless conversions and changed lives. The following account of one of his meetings will give us a glimpse of this power.

I had the flu years ago, and I closed a meeting with the flu racking my body on a Sunday night. I rested a little while Monday morning. But at eleven o'clock Monday morning I got on a train at Winston-Salem and journeyed to Illinois in my flu-weakened condition. I got there about noon on Tuesday and the pastor met me and took me to a room and called a doctor. The pastor told me there wouldn't be many people to hear me preach that night because they were having some sort of an entertainment at the school. While he apologized, the doctor treated me. I went over that night and preached. I must have preached a powerful sermon because all hell broke loose! The chairman of the board of deacons stood out on the steps after the service and raved and raved, and said, "That man is a false prophet and he is going to tear our church up." I didn't know all about this. I had gone back to the room to my sick bed. This deacon said to the pastor, "Here is a check for $400. I will give it to you if you will pay that preacher off and don't let him preach anymore." You know I must have preached a powerful sermon—just one little sermon!

They didn't tell me anything about that and the next night I went over and preached. And it must have been powerful too. I did not understand it, but as soon as I was ready to pronounce the benediction, the pastor said, "I want to meet all the deacons down in the basement." I didn't know what was going on. I slipped out the back door and went back to bed. I was pretty sick. They told me later about how the pastor walked the floor and said, "That preacher is going to ruin us and he is going to tear our church all to pieces," and everybody agreed with him except an old silver haired deacon. When they got around to him, he said, "Boys, you fellows had better let that preacher alone. He is PREACHING THE GOSPEL. You folks have never heard it, and you had better not put your hands on him."

I didn't know about all these things. Thursday night came and the house was just packed and jammed. I wondered what was going on. But unbeknownst to me all of this was going all over the city and here they were coming. Friday night came and the house was packed and jammed. I still didn't know what was going on. Saturday night came, and, lo and behold, the house was crowded and a fellow got up to sing a solo. He didn't mean to do it, but he sang in the power of the Spirit. I saw God take a song, sung in the Spirit, and apply what I had been preaching and pierce hearts with the truth of the gospel. As he stood up there and began to sing, the Holy Ghost took charge of him. He began to sing:

Love sent my Savior to die in my stead,

Why should He love me so?

Meekly to Calvary's cross He was led;

Why should He love me so?

Nails pierced His hands and His feet for my sin,

Why should He love me so?

He suffered sore my salvation to win,

Why should He love me so!

While he was singing all hell began to pop! The organist quit playing and screamed out, "I am lost! I am lost!" That is the sweetest cry that I ever heard this side of eternity. That is the prelude to the cry, "I am saved." She began running to the prayer room. It was the pastor's wife. Then I heard somebody else sobbing, and that poor pastor said, "Oh, my God, I am lost! I'm lost! I'm lost! I'm lost!" And here he ran. Then I saw 14 Roman Catholics. I saw the Sunday school superintendent; I saw seven deacons; I saw (I don't know just how many) as they screamed out before that man could finish his song. They were in the prayer room on their bones sobbing out their souls to God. Because of my preaching? No. because the Holy Spirit took a song, the truth of it, and made this thing personal and brought the truth of the gospel and pierced the hearts of those people. Some people there saw for the first time in their lives that Christ died for them; that He agonized for them; that the nails were put in His hands for them; that He was raised for them.[3]

If we want to have a dynamite faith that has power for ministry and the spread of the gospel then it is imperative we appropriate that dunamis power that is there waiting for us!

---

[3] E. A. Johnston, "God's Hitchhike Evangelist The Biography Of Rolfe Barnard" (Gainesville: Old Paths Publications, 2012), pp 59-61.

The next account I want to share with you is the remarkable ministry of Sam Jones. At the invitation of D. L. Moody, he preached in Chicago in February of 1886 and the account given in the Chicago Tribune reads like the Apostle Paul in the midst of a riot in Ephesus! Remember this report is from a secular newspaper in a major city!

"The Audience last night was large enough, attentive enough, and sufficiently responsive to please the most exciting speaker who ever spoke. There must have been fully nine thousand people packed away in the building. People stood along the aisles on the main floor, stood six and seven deep on the promenade and in the gallery, stood on the stairways, and, in fact, stood everywhere it was possible to stand. There was scarcely breathing much less standing-room. Several hundred people remained in the building from the afternoon service, and by six o'clock nearly every seat was occupied. By half-past six, people were standing, and fifteen minutes later the entrance doors were closed, and no more people were admitted. By seven o'clock there must have been five thousand people massed along State and Twenty-fourth streets, half of them under the impression that the doors had not yet been opened, and the other half believing that, through some providential circumstances they would be able to gain admittance. All the cars going north and south from the Rink were thoroughly packed as if the meeting had just been dismissed, and entirely by people who had despaired of getting into the Casino.

"A careful estimate places the number of people turned away at about ten thousand, really a greater throng than was able to hear the last sermon of this series of revival meetings. The converts began the first week and increasing numbers were added each week. First week were five hundred, second week one thousand, and so on to the end of the five weeks.

"It is a fair estimate that three hundred and fifty thousand heard him in Chicago and twenty-five million read his sermons during the five weeks. No such record is found in all the annals of our Christian religion."[4]

The next example of a dynamite faith is seen in the life and ministry of the great British evangelist, George Whitefield. Whitefield shook two continents for God in powerful revivals! He is considered the greatest British preacher that ever lived. The following account is a good example of his powerful ministry whose main message was, "Ye must be born again."

George Whitefield preached in the open air to upwards of thirty thousand people at time. In fact, his good friend in Philadelphia, Ben Franklin, estimated while walking among an outdoor crowd assembled to hear Whitefield preach in Philadelphia, with pen and paper in hand, counting groups of fifties, Franklin estimated that Whitefield could be easily heard by thirty thousand people.

During the Great Awakening George Whitefield preached to Jonathan Edwards'

---

[4] E. A. Johnston, "Sam Jones A New Biography" (Gainesville: Old Paths Publications, 2023), pp 161-162.

congregation in Northhampton, MA , and we have this description from a letter by Sarah Edwards, Jonathan Edwards' wife:

> "It is wonderful to see what a spell he casts over an audience by proclaiming the simple truths of the Bible. I have seen upwards of a thousand people hang on his words with breathless silence, broken only by an occasional half-suppressed sob. He impresses the ignorant, and not less the educated and refined. It is reported that while the miners of England listened to him, the tears made white furrows down their smutty cheeks. So here, our mechanics shut up their shops, and the day-laborers throw down their tools, to go and hear him preach, and few return unaffected...He speaks from a heart all aglow with love, and pours out a torrent of eloquence which is almost irresistible. Many, very many persons in Northhampton date the

beginning of new thoughts, new desires, new purposes, and a new life, from the day on which they heard him preach of Christ and this salvation."[5]

---

[5] E. A. Johnston, "George Whitefield A Definitive Biography Two Volumes in One" (Gainesville: Old Paths Publications, 2024) Volume One, p 403

CHAPTER SEVENTEEN
THE MAKING OF A MAN OF FAITH

"In the courtyard of denial, where Peter denied his Master three times, we read in the Gospel of Luke: *"And the Lord turned, and looked upon Peter"* (Luke 22:61). This was not a look of disapproval, nor of disappointment, Jesus already had foretold Peter's denial of Him. No, the look on Christ's face, as He gazed into Peter's eyes, was a look of encouragement—for when Jesus looked at Peter He did not see the bumbling, stumbling, wishy-washy disciple; rather, when Jesus looked on Peter, in Peter's deepest hour of failure, what He saw was the Peter of Pentecost preaching the house down with authority and power and adding three thousand souls to the church! For when Jesus looks at YOU, He doesn't see your faults and failures, rather He sees the PERSON THAT YOU WILL BECOME!"

E. A. JOHNSTON

FAITH LESSON: The Making of a Man of Faith

BIBLE PASSAGE: Judges 6:12

It is incredible how God can take an ordinary man, a plain man, and change and transform that man into a new man who He can use for His great glory! D. L. Moody comes to mind. Moody was a rough, uneducated man who could not properly spell the word "bed"; yet God made D. L. Moody into a mighty instrument in His hand to where Moody held the attention of 10,000 people at a time for a month at a time in major metropolises of London, Edinburgh, and Glasgow. The making of a man of faith is one of the greatest studies in our Bibles because it demonstrates to us personally what our own possibilities are in the kingdom of God when a dynamite God gets a hold of us and fills us with His power!

ur FAITH LESSON for today is about Gideon "the man of valor". We read in Judges chapter six:

"And the children of Israel did evil in the sight of the LORD: and the LORD delivered them into the hand of Midian seven years" (Judges 6:1).

Israel in the days of Gideon was a time of great apostasy in the people of God. The Jews were in a "sin-cycle" where Israel falls into apostasy and God would send an oppressor in the form of a remedial judgement; Israel would repent, and God sends a deliverer, then there is peace and prosperity until the people fall into gross sin once more and the cycle is repeated. Out of this dark backdrop we come across a ray of light in the form of a man called Gideon. Gideon is in the "Hall of Faith" in Hebrews chapter eleven; but he wasn't always a man of faith—God had to make him a man of faith.

We are introduced to Gideon in Judges 6:11, where we find a plain ordinary man threshing wheat. But what is remarkable about this man Gideon is his visitor: *"And there came an angel of the LORD, and sat under an oak which was in Ophrah, that pertained unto Joash the Abi-ezrite: and his son Gideon threshed wheat by the winepress, to hide it from the Midianites."*

The foreign oppressors were stealing crops and eating everything in sight. God steps out of heaven in the form of a theophany, an angel of the Lord and appears to Gideon. *"And the angel of the LORD appeared unto him, and said unto him, The LORD is with thee, thou mighty man of valor"* (Judges 6:12).

Then we see how Gideon sees himself.

> *"And the LORD looked upon him, and said, Go in this thy might, and thou shalt save Israel from the hand of the Midianites: have not I sent thee? And he said unto him, Oh my Lord, wherewith shall I save Israel? behold, my family is poor in Manasseh, and I*

am the least in my father's house"
(Judges 6:14-15).

Now, is Gideon presently a mighty warrior and conqueror? No, he is a mere lad, least in this father's house—like David the shepherd boy was. But God sees him as WHO HE WILL BECOME—A MAN OF FAITH THAT HE CAN USE! But first, God must make Gideon into a man of faith. We see this process in the following accounts:

1. The angel of the LORD asks Gideon to perform a task, to prepare a sacrifice of a kid and unleavened cakes and Gideon follows the instructions to the letter (v 20) and this is a FIRST STEP OF FAITH and that is OBEDIENCE.
2. Then the angel asks Gideon to destroy the altar of Baal (verses 25-27). The SECOND STEP OF FAITH IS PERFORMING A DANGEROUS TASK FOR GOD THAT MAY HAVE REPERCUSSIONS. The town people were upset at Gideon for destroying the altar of Baal and they went into a mob riot to put him to death (verses 30-31).

3. The NEXT STEP OF FAITH IS ASKING GOD TO PERFORM A SUPERNATURAL ACT TO DEMONSTRATE HIS POWER. We see this as Gideon prepares for battle and he wants confidence in God's help, so he puts the fleece of wool out: "And Gideon said unto God, If will save Israel by mine hand, as thou hast said, Behold, I will put a fleece of wool in the floor; and if the dew be on the fleece only, and if it be dry upon all the earth beside, then shall I know that thou wilt save Israel by mine hand, as thou hast said" (Judges 6:36-37). God performs this miracle for Gideon. But Gideon's faith is little here and he needs more evidence before he can trust God more fully. "And Gideon said unto God, Let not thine anger be hot against me, and I will speak but this once: let me prove, I pray thee, but this once with the fleece; let it now be dry only upon the fleece, and upon all the ground let there be dew" (Judges 6:39). God was building faith in His servant gradually—as He does with each of us as well.

4. The NEXT STEP OF FAITH IS MORE SEVERE. GIDEON'S FAITH IS

STRETCHED TO STRENGTHEN HIS FAITH AND TO KNOW HIS RELIANCE IS UPON GOD AND NOT MEN. The Midianite army numbered 135,000 men. Gideon's army numbered 32,000 men. The enemies of God outnumbered Gideon's army four to one! But God wants Gideon to go against the Midianites with only a mere 300 men! God chooses His soldiers by picking men who lapped the water (7:5-6). God's object lesson to Gideon's faith is to avoid any self-reliance on human strength and effort. God is teaching Gideon the principle from Zechariah 4:6, "Then he answered and spake unto me saying, This is the word of the LORD unto Zerubbabel, saying, Not by might, nor by power, but by my Spirit saith the LORD of hosts." Gideon goes on to a great victory with his 300 men! He is learning that God is a dynamite God who has power to save! And we see this young man become the "man of valor." Just like God called him!

The making of a man of faith is a process, a slow painful process. God is able to make the man of faith. Our part is to be

AVAILABLE to be TEACHABLE through our OBEDIENCE and TRUST in God to let Him do the necessary work in us so we can become the PERSON HE KNOWS WE CAN BE!

CHAPTER EIGHTEEN
RECOMMENDED READING

The following list of books on faith are suggested because they have built faith in me. When I led my first discipleship group back in the early 1990's, one of the studies for that group of men was the *"Men of Faith Series"* books published by Penguin. These were inexpensive paperbacks that gave us a rich resource to read about men of faith. Other suggested books on faith are as follows:

1. *C. T. Studd*, by Norman Grubb
2. *Rees Howells, Intercessor,* by Norman Grubb
3. *John Sung's Diaries* by Levi
4. *The Memoirs of Charles Finney*, by Charles Finney
5. *A Definitive Biography of George Whitefield,* two volumes in one, paperback, by E. A. Johnston
6. *Sam Jones A New Biography,* by E. A. Johnston
7. *Asahel Nettleton: Revival Preacher*, by E. A. Johnston, paperback

8. *God's Hitchhike Evangelist: The Biography of Rolfe Barnard*, E. A. Johnston

ABOUT THE AUTHOR

E.A. Johnston in the Outdoor pulpit at Hanham Mount where George Whitefield preached, courtesy of Digby James.

E. A. Johnston, Ph.D., D. B. S., is a Fellow with the Stephen Olford Institute for Biblical Preaching and is an evangelist and author with eighteen published books. He is the founder of Evangelism Awakening, a revival-based ministry whose focus is the study of historical revival and preaching for revival in our day. He has over two thousand sermons on SermonAudio.com.

SOME OF THE BOOKS BY E. A. JOHNSTON

Many of the following books may be purchased individually or as a set by going to Dr. Johnston's webpage in the bookstore at The Old Paths Publications that has links to distributors. Go to:

www.theoldpathspublications.com/Pages/Authors/Johnston.htm

1. *"A Heart Awake: The Authorized Biography of J. Sidlow Baxter"* Foreword by Adrian Rogers (The Old Paths Publications, www.theoldpathspublications.com).

2. *"Realities Of Revival"* Foreword by Stephen F. Olford (Gospel Folio Press, Canada; 2005).

3. *"No Turning Back"* (Gospel Folio Press, Canada; 2005).

4. *"The Master's Plan: Unfolding God's Blueprint For Your Life"* (Gospel Folio Press, Canada; 2006).

5. *"Know The Book: Bible Survey At A Glance"* (Gospel Folio Press, Canada; 2007).

6. *"Jua Kitabu: Tazamo la Biblia" Know The Book* translated into the Swahili by missionary G. I. Harlow (Everyday Publications, Canada; 2007).

7. *"Walking With God"* Foreword by Ted S. Rendall (Gospel Folio Press, Canada; 2007).

8. *"Return To Me: Entering A Right Relationship With God"* (Gospel Folio Press, Canada; 2007).

9. *"Are You In The Book Of Life?"* (Gospel Folio Press, Canada; 2008).

10. *"Call To Revival"* Foreword By Colin Peckham (Gospel Folio Press, Canada; 2008).

11. *"The Church In Revival"* Foreword By Richard Owen Roberts (Gospel Folio Press, Canada; 2008).

12. *"Olford On Scroggie: Stephen Olford's Notes on the Sermon Outlines of Graham*

Scroggie" Co-authored with Stephen Olford (The Old Paths Publications: www.theoldpathspublications.com).

13. *"George Whitefield A Definitive Biography, Volumes 1 and 2 Combined"* (The Old Paths Publications: www.theoldpathspublications.com).

14. *"George Whitefield A Definitive Biography In Two Volumes"* (American edition published by Revival Literature, Asheville; 2012).

15. *"God's Hitchhike Evangelist The Biography Of Rolfe Barnard"* Foreword By Bob Doom (The Old Paths Publications: www.theoldpathspublications.com).

16. *"Asahel Nettleton Revival Preacher"* Foreword By John Thornbury, Preface By Richard Owen Roberts (The Old Paths Publications: www.theoldpathspublications.com).

17. *"Sermons For Revival"* (The Old Paths Publications: www.theoldpathspublications.com).

18. *"A Noble Company Biographical Essays on Notable Particular Baptists in*

America Volume 11: Portrait of Rolfe Barnard" (Particular Baptist Press, Springfield; 2018).

19. *"Lectures On Revival For A Laodicean Church,"* (The Old Paths Publications, www.theoldpathspublications.com)

20. *"Sam Jones, A New Biography"* (The Old Paths Publications: www.theoldpathspublications.com)

21. E. A. Johnston's Book Set, (The Old Paths Publications, www.theoldpathspublications.com (30% off retail)

Many of these books can be purchased in The Old Paths Publications Bookstore at a discounted price. Go here:

https://www.theoldpathspublications.com/Pages/BookStore.htm